The New Adventure Playground Movement:

How Communities across the USA are Returning Risk and Freedom to Childhood

By

Morgan Leichter-Saxby and Suzanna Law
of Pop-Up Adventure Play

Notebook|Publishing

First published in the UK in 2015 by Notebook Publishing, 145–157 St John Street, London, EC1V 4PW.

www.notebookpublishing.co.uk

ISBN: 9780956553997

Typeset by Notebook Publishing
Printed and bound in Great Britain

ACKNOWLEDGEMENTS

A huge thank you to the hosts, funders and participants of the tour, Pop-Up Adventure Play's Board members, and our friends and family for their support. Thank you to Hayley Paige of Notebook Publishing for her expertise and generosity in getting this book into your hands.

'Avoiding danger in the long run is no safer than outright exposure. Life is either a daring adventure or it is nothing.'
(Helen Keller)

'If you never did, you should. These things are fun, and fun is good.'
(Dr Seuss)

INTRODUCTION

CHILDREN AND PLAY

Children play everywhere they go—usually until they're told not to. They're growing in a world full of excitement; however, opportunities to explore are often cut short by parents or teachers who never expected to spend so much of their days saying 'no'. Adults often have fond memories of their own youthful escapades: jumping over the back fence to meet friends or maybe going for bike rides on their own. Previous generations had the chance to discover that the best playgrounds are often not playgrounds at all, but vacant spaces overgrown with a jungle of weeds, or abandoned building sites. These are the places children have always gone when they wanted *adventures*—especially the kinds of adventure parents aren't supposed to know about. Sadly, however, chances are becoming more and more difficult for children to find.

We believe that every child *knows* how to play, and needs only time, space, opportunity and maybe a little support in order to do so. Climbing trees, making box forts, loitering in hammocks—these are the experiences every child needs and deserves.

We hear again and again that 'times are different today' and that children can't have the freedom previous generations took for granted. Children need supervision and protection, and their parents need to be reassured that a little risk is perfectly safe.

Adventure playgrounds are one response to this problem.

A SHORT HISTORY OF ADVENTURE PLAYGROUNDS

C. Th. Sorensen was a Danish landscape and playground designer, who noticed one day in 1931 that children liked to play everywhere *but* on the conventional fixed playground equipment—in particular, they loved playing in building sites—so he proposed a place full of wood, hammers, nails, shovels and dirt. He called it 'a junk playground in which children could create and shape, dream and imagine a reality' (Bosselmann, 1998), and imagined it would help city children to enjoy the experiences those children in the countryside took for granted.

It took until 1943, in Nazi-occupied Copenhagen, for that vision to become a reality.

The first member of staff was John Bertelsen, who explained that his role was not to educate or guide: 'I cannot, and indeed will not, teach the children anything. I am able to give them my support in their creative play and work, and thus help them in developing those talents and abilities which are often suppressed at home and at school. I consider it most important that the leader not appear *too clever* but that he remain at the same experimental stage as the children. In this way the initiative is left, to a great extent, with the children themselves and it is thus far easier to avoid serious intrusion into their fantasy world' (1972, pp. 20–21).

An estimated nine hundred children attended the first day. Over time, they constructed an elaborate and changing city of their own, complete with towers and lookouts, fortresses, tunnels and more. Lady Allen of Hurtwood, a landscape architect, pacifist and children's welfare advocate, visited Emdrup and was enchanted.

At the time, the UK was grieving and exhausted by war. Bombing had flattened whole districts. 'Operation Pied Piper' evacuated 1.9 million children from the heavily bombed cities to live with strangers in the countryside—in some cases, for years—before returning them to a changed world. Rationing continued until 1954, with sweets and sugars the last to be deregulated. Amidst all of this, children played. For Lady Allen, it seemed so obvious: if children were already playing in bomb sites, 'why not make some of them safe places to play in?' (Bengtsson, 1972, p. 25). This question was put forward in a popular magazine called the *Picture Post*, which featured Lady Allen's campaign in favour of these newly renamed 'adventure playgrounds', alongside moving images of children literally building new cities from the rubble.

A wave of interest in the 1960s and 1970s emphasised the aspect of children's self-government. Colin Ward, British Anarchist and author of *Child in the City* (1978), argued that a good adventure playground functioned as 'a free society in miniature, with the same tensions and ever-changing harmonies, the same diversity and spontaneity, the same unforced growth of co-operation and release of individual qualities and communal sense, which lie dormant in a society whose dominant values are competition and acquisitiveness' (Ward, 1982, pp. 90–91). Practitioners published their experiences and accordingly gathered theory from a range of disciplines, developing the foundation of the playwork profession.

The early 2000s witnessed another wave, this time in a snowball of large-scale funding. Play Wales released the Playwork Principles in 2004, with the national training body providing its endorsement the following year. In 2008, the Secretary of State for Children, Schools and Families, Ed Balls, tried out the homemade swings on an adventure playground before announcing the world's first ever national government play strategy (DCSF, 2008). He had £235m of new treasury funding for first three years, and put play the heart of a 12-year plan to make England 'the best place in the world to grow up'. Playworkers expanded their field of operations to include schools, hospitals, public space and anywhere else children can be found. Some of these are known as 'play rangers' owing to the fact they operate across a local landscape, fostering the social connections that enable children to play outside freely.

Today, playwork courses are taught at approximately sixty different UK-based further education institutions, as part of degrees up to PhD level. There are an estimated 50,000 playworkers in the UK, and every year some are honoured at the National Playwork Conference (Meynell Games, 2015).

However, the combination of global financial collapse and a coalition government has resulted in funding being stripped from play at all levels. Good adventure playgrounds have been closed at a record pace, while others have managed to 'survive' by transforming to something more like childcare. There are still a handful of wonderful adventure playgrounds, staunchly defended by staff and local residents. Many practitioners are applying these skills elsewhere, or as volunteers and activists from within neighbouring fields, while others are sharing their experiences online, and are often surprised to discover the international interest in adventure playgrounds.

ADVENTURE PLAYGROUNDS IN THE USA

Trying to learn about the adventure playground movement in the US involves a great deal of rumour. 'I've heard of one in Portland,' someone will say at a conference, whereas others will mention New York City or Southern California, but can't remember quite where they heard that.

In *Grounds for Play* (1974), Joe Benjamin describes a project in 1950 Minneapolis that aimed at stimulating creative play so that the children could learn the basic process of living while playing. Children were provided with 'second-hand materials of all kinds', and signed out lots, allowing them to embark on their own projects. The project lasted for one year, but does not seem to have been well documented. In *Adventure Playgrounds* (1972), Bengtsson tells of an adventure playground in Boston, known as the Lenox-Camden Playground in 1966.

According to Joe Frost's authoritative 2010 work, *A History of Children's Play and Play Environments*, the American Adventure Playground Association (AAPA) reported a total of sixteen adventure playgrounds in the US in 1977. We spoke with Halcyon Learned, formerly part of the Houston Adventure Playground Association (HAPA), who said that, at one point, the city had three sites, built underneath freeway overpasses so that no one complained about the noise. The last one closed in 1997—and HAPA along with it.

A handful of sites from the era remain: Mercer Island Adventure Playground in Seattle, plus two in California (Berkeley Adventure

Playground, and Huntington Beach Adventure Playground). Two more (the AP at the Parish School in Houston, TX and the Hands-on-Nature Anarchy Zone in Ithaca, NY) draw on the adventure playground model to do something slightly different, as you'll see in these pages.

Today, new sites are in the process of forming *at this very moment.* We are confident in calling this a growing movement; in fact, Suzanna is currently pursuing a PhD on this very issue! By this, we mean that there is a growing number of people who are dissatisfied with the issue of children's lack of opportunities to play. Social movements tend to focus on the barriers faced changing or overcoming a problematic situation; in this instance, this infers discussing and addressing adult perceptions of fear (stranger danger), as well as the pressures of standardised tests (political policy), all of which prevent play from occurring. This social movement is relatively new in its current form; thus, the barriers between children and the opportunities they need are still being identified, with supporting evidence still being gathered. Studies have demonstrated repeatedly that children need play to learn and grow, thrive and participate; evidence of need and examples of best practice are essential tools used by advocates for children's right to play. Another useful tool for many practitioners is the United Nation's Convention on the Rights of the Child. First signed in 1989, it has been signed by more countries than any other UN Convention, and specifically includes 'the right to rest and leisure, to engage in play and recreational activities'. To date, it has been signed by every member state other than South Sudan (unable to sign due to a lack of recognised government) and the USA.

PLAYWORK PRACTICE

As has been shown thus far, playwork has grown and blossomed out of the adventure playground movement, but now includes people working in different arenas. These professionals are connected by a set of formal Playwork Principles (Appendix), as well as a certain outlook. Dr Fraser Brown (Professor of Playwork at Leeds Beckett University), explains, 'playworkers should adopt a non-judgmental, non-prejudicial, non-directive, and largely reflective approach to their work' (Brown, 2008). In many cases, this involves creating a safe and flexible environment within which children can be free, and then deliberately *letting go* of our adult assumptions and expectations regarding what they might do there. The best play sites are always evolving, led by the needs and desires of the children who attend, with adults being careful to respond to children's cues and to withdraw when no longer needed.

One key aspect of playwork is the focus on children's own, self-directed play as our top priority. We spend a lot of time thinking about the *environments* of play, always seeking ways to 'loosen them up' so that children can take, shape and transform whatever they can find into whatever they might need. For us, many of the problems children face today (such as aggression, anxiety and depression) can be framed as symptoms of play deprivation.

The field of playwork is far larger than can be addressed here; becoming a playworker takes time, education, practice and the support of a good team. There is some more information on routes into this field, provided at the end of this book, and our website provides a wealth of tips on how to apply the basics of playwork in any setting.

Unquestionably, playwork is a challenging approach with the potential to be astonishingly rewarding. It involves a great deal of work behind the scenes and training in tools such as risk/benefit assessments. When studying playwork, new practitioners find a whole new vocabulary for discussing what they see and how children behave in the space. It is a position that asks adults to take a great deal of responsibility, while at the same time reminding them to remain humble and learn from the play experts in our care.

POP-UP ADVENTURE PLAY

The original idea of a pop-up adventure playground was based on the idea that play is good for everyone. We wanted to incorporate as much of the classic adventure playground as possible, while also directing efforts towards making it easy for communities to build themselves. By using materials already possessed, along with the public space shared with their neighbours, organisers have been hosting events that welcome everyone *and* give them something to talk about afterwards. We held the first pop-up adventure playground in New York City in 2010, and very soon people began to email from around the world—Boston, Bogota, Cairo, Mexico City and Shanghai. Again and again, these individuals shared the same concerns: parents working too hard, children under academic pressure, and crumbling social networks—all contributing to one key problem: children not playing out the way they used to. Furthermore, this situation reproduces itself: when people feel surrounded by strangers, they don't feel confident making new friends. They report feeling less safe in their own neighbourhoods, and more alone. Children playing outside are both the symptom and catalyst of a healthy society: their presence in public space demonstrates community networks while strengthening them.

This provided the foundation for our design of the pop-up adventure playground model. These events are free, public celebrations of child-directed play, filled with ordinary and recycled materials (such as cardboard boxes, fabric, tape and string), with adults ready to support play without providing direction. They offer a 'starter' version of the classic adventure playground model, gently introducing themes of risk and freedom by welcoming and encouraging people of all ages and abilities to play together. We always urge new organisers to start small and grow from within their community of support, building the skills necessary for a more permanent site as they go. For many of the organisers you'll meet here, pop-up adventure playgrounds are gateway projects, building towards a permanent site. Others view pop-up adventure playgrounds as a way to reach out into communities they don't often see, or to collaborate with other local institutions or festivals.

Every independent organiser gets a free resource pack filled with useful tips and the beginnings of playwork training—both from us, and from the experience itself. We also offer professional development workshops, staff training, site evaluations and more, travelling to be of use wherever we are invited. So far, there are independent organisers in more than a dozen countries worldwide, including the USA, Australia, Canada, Costa Rica, Colombia and Uganda.

THIS BOOK

Most of the people you'll meet here have run pop-up adventure playgrounds of their own, and many are students on our Playworker Development Course—an online course in playwork developed for international learners. This reflects our own bias because, of course, we chose to visit and write about people with whom we are already connected. It would be impossible to mention everyone doing great work in the USA; instead, this book is intended to provide a snapshot of this movement at a particular moment in time, as seen during one road trip.

We hope these pages inspire and motivate you, and at the very least prove that wonderful things are happening in children's lives all over this country. It is easy to become pessimistic, but let this book prove that there are dedicated, clever people working hard to change how people view risk and freedom. Undoubtedly, it is a big job, and we'd like to acknowledge the kindness and encouragement of those we've met who remember previous waves of adventure playground enthusiasm, and survived its lulls.

One such individual is Professor Robin Moore, who, for decades, has been working in the early childhood field. He came to our pop-up in North Carolina and stood to one side, watching two children experiment with a seesaw they'd built out of cardboard tubes and duct tape. We'd been talking about a shift we'd each felt recently, a sense of momentum growing in support of play. He turned to us and said, 'I have worked in the US for over 20 years, and this is the most hopeful I have felt about the future of play for a long time'.

"I have worked in the US for 20 years, and this is the most hopeful I have felt about the future of play in a long time."
Robin Moore

STORY OF THE TOUR

BY SUZANNA

The tour seems like so long ago. In fact, it seems a little bit like a dream to me; a two-month long dream, shared by only one other person. And when I stare in disbelief at some of the images from our trip, I like to webcam with Morgan and stare at her, too; I can't quite believe we drove for almost 11,000 miles in the tiniest yellow car imaginable.

And what, you might ask, was the reason for such an incredible journey? Well, we were responding to need. We were responding to the requests from all over the USA from people who wanted to find out more about play, more about playwork, and more about how play can change their lives. We were invited into communities just as a playworker is invited into play, and in return we were deeply inspired by these amazing people.

As I flick through the photos, I see the faces of 16 hosts that took us into their homes, fed us at their kitchen tables, and spoke of their hopes and dreams for play. That's 16 little groups of people in 16 different locations across the USA—exactly double the number of our original aim. Double. There were folks who we have worked with before, groups with whom we'd been in conversation with for a long time, and new friends who reached out to us for the very first time. Actually, location number 16 was booked two weeks into the tour upon hearing that we would be heading their way!

We were enormously humbled to meet these play champions in their own communities as they spoke about their work, their passion for play, and their isolation from others in the field. As we crossed 28 State lines, we reflected on just how important our tour mission was: to connect play people from across the country with other like-minded people in order to inspire communities to take a step forward in the confidence that play would lift their community as they work together. We were invited into communities to meet their needs, and together with some of our Special Guest friends, their needs were met through play.

Upon arriving at each site, we delivered workshops introducing the basic ideas of playwork. Working closely with the hosts, we tailored each of these to meet the needs of the community, and included time for the participants to play. There are so many great photos of adults at play, capturing moments in my mind that I recall fondly, and of course abundant photos of Pop-Up Adventure Playgrounds that we helped to run as part of the tour.

So many memories, so many great play moments.

It was an incredible journey that started with two playworkers in one little car, and ended with a reach of over 2,000 people spanning 30 events. But that's just the beginning...

Welcome to this story, and thank you for picking up this book. You, too, are now a part of the adventure.

PLAY HOT YALL

THE TOUR IN FIGURES

THE TOUR'S VITAL STATISTICS

Dates: February 19, 2014–April 19, 2014

Miles: Almost 11,000

Greatest Height: 8,000 ft. above sea level

Top speed: 94 mph

List of locations: Berkshire MA, Ithaca NY, Louisville KY, Houston TX, Newhall CA, Manhattan Beach CA, San Diego CA, Seattle WA, Portland OR, Chicago IL, Port Clinton OH, Raleigh NC, Buffalo NY, Philadelphia PA, Lakeville MA, Brookline MA.

Estimated number of participants: 2,000+

External financial support:

Crowdfunding: $3,547.28

Grant from Kaboom: $2,500.00

Other donations: $295.00.

Funds were raised through professional development grants, ticketed events and by donation. Public pop-up adventure playgrounds were free of charge and open to all.

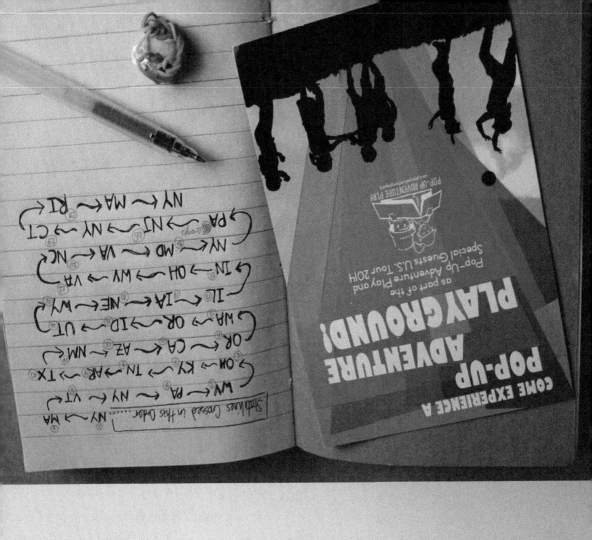
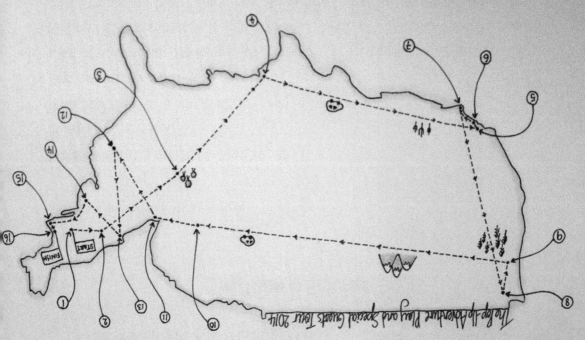

STAFF PROFILES

Name: Suzanna Law

Tour Responsibility: Tour Coordinator, Technology Operator and Advisor

Favourite Tour Moment: 'Feeding the llamas at a gas station—the only building for miles—in the hills of Wyoming, 7,000 ft. above sea level!'

Bios: With more than 7 years' experience in the playwork field, Suzanna took the lead in organising and heading the tour, which worked perfectly with the Playwork PhD in which she is currently enrolled at Leeds Beckett University. Based in the UK, Suzanna worked closely with each of the US location hosts, communicating via both email and telephone, and skilfully publicised the tour through social media and newsletters to Pop-Up Adventure Play's global network of contacts.

Name: Morgan Leichter-Saxby

Tour Responsibility: Vehicle Acquisition, Navigation and Control, Workshop Leader

Favourite Tour Moment: 'Getting the car stuck inside a giant redwood, and slooooowly driving through it with a loud scraping noise!'

Bio: Morgan first visited an adventure playground as an anthropologist in 2007, looking for fieldwork sites. She immediately started training as a playworker, focusing on fixed and ranging projects across London. Since then, Morgan has travelled to ten countries and spoken at over a dozen international conferences, including as Keynote Speaker at the 2013 International Children's Development Forum in Bogota. As resident American in the little yellow car, Morgan was our very own tour guide, and took the lead on delivering workshops. She is now working on her PhD in playwork at Leeds Beckett University.

SPECIAL GUESTS

Name: Grant Lambie

Expertise: Slow Build Adventure Playgrounds

Favourite Tour Moment: 'After stopping for a vegetarian pizza (which the shop hadn't made for some time because no one knew it was on the menu) on the way to Kentucky, on the other side of the road were these amazing, surreal slides, with beautiful snow-covered hills in the background.'

Bio: Grant has spent 26 years in London's parks, schools and public housing projects, opening new natural playscapes and revitalising old ones. Designing new play structures that are child- and community-led, designed and built is central to Grant's belief in the importance of providing children and young people with a sense of ownership of these spaces. Grant was the tour's expert on the 'slow build' approach, which offers fluid and dynamic methods for direct community engagement as part of an ever-evolving process.

Name: Andy Hinchcliffe

Expertise: Play in the Community

Favourite Tour Moment: 'Somewhere over the rainbow, way up in Fort Bragg, California, we stumbled upon a peculiar, albeit charming, diner, which could have easily drawn out a dimpled smile from the most wilful of frowns. We'd reached 'Oz'—inclusive of its very own 'Yellow Brick Road', which, after humorous instruction from the owner, led us to the privy of all privies.... The 'Emerald City Toilets'! What a strange but unexpected pleasure!'

Bio: Andy is Manager of a play-centred community and children's centre in a neighbourhood of profound socio-economic deprivation. Their play area functions as an adventure playground. Having graduated from Leeds Beckett University with top grades in Playwork, Andy is considering further study in this arena. On the tour, he provided expertise on community integration and social cohesion.

Name: Erin Davis

Expertise: Documentation and film

Favourite Tour Moment: 'It was so exciting to see footage from *The Land* projected for the first time. Oversized and projected onto a gently billowing sheet, the footage flickered with life.'

Bio: Erin is an artist, filmmaker, radio producer and educator living in Vermont, USA. Her adventure playground documentary, *The Land*, is out this year. Her unique take on adventure playgrounds and special talents in documentation made her an invaluable part of the tour.

CHAPTER ONE

I was born in California, and lived in Vermont and New York for many years. My family is in San Diego and outside of Boston, and until this tour I was a bi-coastal cliché.

When we first settled into the little yellow car, I prepped Suzanna with a crash course in terminology, including concepts such as red states and blue states, as well as 'real' America and coastal snobbery. She took a moment to, once again, consider the scale of our undertaking.

'How many states have you been to?' she asked me.

I thought for a moment, counting up visits to family members and a post-college road trip. 'If you don't count when I was very small, maybe 12? But hardly anywhere beyond the coasts.'

'How many have most people been to?'

I shrugged. 'No idea. Many people will have seen more, and probably a lot will have seen fewer.'

There was a long pause.

'How many will we go through on this trip?' I asked.

She considered. 'Twenty-something?'

My brain short-circuited.

She looked at me from the driver's seat and grinned. 'That's if we don't get lost.'

I was so curious about the landscape and towns we'd pass through, feeling the next two months of our lives roll along before us like a carpet. More than anything, I was curious about the people we'd meet. We knew a little about the hosts already, if only that they cared about children's play, had been seeking out information online, *and* were willing to work with at least two total strangers! Many of them had become friends through email, but building those relationships had been Suzanna's lookout. During the planning stages, she'd phone with questions like, 'How far apart are Portland and Chicago, really?', and I'd answer that it was quite far and mention other things, such as blizzards.

To help us cover this impossible-seeming distance, I'd been assigned the task of finding a car.

Our original vision included a converted school bus we could sleep aboard with an elegant storage arrangement. Suzanna looked at gas averages and motel prices, and I set off to the dealership with hopes of a Subaru Outback. Instead (and after having asked Suzanna's opinion), I ended up signing on the dotted line for a tiny Chevrolet Aveo, telling myself that British people are used to small cars. The only thing it shared with our first idea was the colour—a bright, cheery yellow. I bought a large plastic roof box via Craigslist, and that nearly doubled its size.

When Suzanna arrived, we went to practice driving manoeuvers in the parking lot of a closed-down Walmart outside of town. She dodged the piles of snow, getting used to shifting gears with her other hand. 'On the right, the *right*,' she whispered. After, we headed back in the dying daylight to put on the roof box, our fingers burning with cold. Suzanna climbed up into the box itself to hold the final bolt, and I stood beneath her, arms out as she slithered down. Go, playworkers!

We had a large map of the country marked with our destinations in purple pencil, and a GPS Suzanna introduced as 'Rhonda'. Andy, a tour guest and UK board member, had sent two huge magnetic stickers with our logo, and we carefully stuck them on the doors. The car contained everything we believed to be necessary, from wool coats to sunscreen, and we were picking up Grant at an airport en-route. The roof box was filled with cardboard tubes, the gas tank was full, and, most importantly, we had snacks. We were off!

STARTING SMALL AND GROWING

Tickets to our talks were being sold long in advance of our arrival. Hosts explained that there would be teachers and childcare workers, parks and recreation staff, therapists, landscape architects and more. It seemed clear that the audience for a discussion around play, freedom, risk and community was already very diverse. However, for many of them, the phrase 'adventure playground' meant only one thing—Plas Madoc or 'The Land' in Wrexham, North Wales. It was featured in *The Atlantic* and on National Public Radio, largely thanks to Erin Davis's new documentary, *The Land*. Erin Davis joined us in Philadelphia, sharing some footage and stories from the shoot.

'The playground is laid out in a way that you enter through a gate and walk through a passage about as wide as a hallway. You walk down a short slope, then the space opens up as you walk up a slight hill and into the playground. It's all outside…

'As I walked through the passage and started to make my way up the hill, I felt immediately dwarfed by a tall tree here, a baby doll head there, and really had the sensation of having passed through a threshold. I think I had the camera rolling during that moment and it's totally unwatchable. I was completely distracted and everything is shaky; the sound is out of whack. I was just totally stimulated by the world and unable to focus on the filming for those first moments as I acclimated to the space.'

This wasn't always the case. The site opened in 2012, and Claire Griffiths, the Senior Playworker, was initially concerned that children would be disappointed by its spartan beginning. They'd toured other, more established adventure playgrounds together, and she thought they'd expect a zip line, tree houses and more to be already installed and available. 'But in the end,' she said, gesturing to the houses built from pallets and the swings that flew over a stream, 'we just put the fence around it and let them go.

They built it, and I was so glad we trusted them.'

When adults first fall in love with the idea of an adventure playground, with the hand-built towers and bonfires, it's easy to let that vision get in the way of observing how children are playing in the space already. There's nothing wrong with 'just' digging for a while because the actual point of an adventure playground isn't risk or construction, but *freedom*—which is partly why we advise pop-up adventure playground organisers to use 'non-threatening' construction materials, such as cardboard boxes: it helps them to say to children 'you're free to play here' and really mean it.

Regardless of the materials or site in mind, however, we always advise people to start small. Whether you're hosting an event or delivering a speech, there's always a shivery little moment before people arrive. '*What if no one comes?*' people wonder. Then, as people start arriving, '*What if everybody comes?*'

All we can suggest is this: trust in the process is rewarded.

KEY PLAYERS

Tricia O'Connor: Lake Erie Adventure Play, Port Clinton, OH

Tricia built a career working in children's museums, for years maintaining at the back of her mind the notion of adventure playgrounds. 'Nothing ever came of it,' she mentioned, 'until we moved to a small community in northern Ohio for my husband's new job'. That town is Port Clinton—made famous by Dr Robert Putnam (author of *Bowling Alone: The Collapse and Revival of American Community*) shortly after their arrival—which was recognised as the 'poster child of the crumbling American dream'.

'The article cited staggering levels of childhood poverty (50%) and a breakdown in the social structure as an example of what's happening in communities across the United States. After a town hall meeting, our local United Way director put out a call for volunteers. 'Is there anyone here who can do anything to help our kids?' she asked, and I said, 'Me. I can'. Melissa Bayer, a Montessori teacher and fellow adventure playground enthusiast, had also volunteered. And so, with the support of United Way, together they started delivering pop-up adventure playgrounds and other community-based play services around the Port Clinton area under the name LEAP (Lake Erie Adventure Play).

'We started in what we call our mobile mode; going into neighbourhoods (especially low-income neighbourhoods) and festivals, setting up our materials and supporting kids and grownups as they play. Pop-ups are how we've started—they're low-cost for us, low-liability for the community (sometimes adventure playgrounds look a little frightening to community leaders) because we use child-safe materials, and they're helping us build a groundswell of community support.'

What's more, Tricia feels she's benefited personally from the experience:

'I have loved learning more ways to support children's play without directing it. I had a great time playing outdoors as a kid, mostly away from the eyes of adults, and figuring things out as we went along and having such wonderful adventures. I've wanted my whole life to offer that back to kids. Since I never had kids of my own, something I really really wanted, this is finally giving me the chance. Plus, I have a ton of fun. I'm get to play, too ... and we all need play. This gives me license to do so - I get to be crazy and silly too, even at 53!'

At the time of writing, Tricia and Melissa are hard at work, delivering loose parts play services from a donated SUV, and have their eye on a promising piece of land...

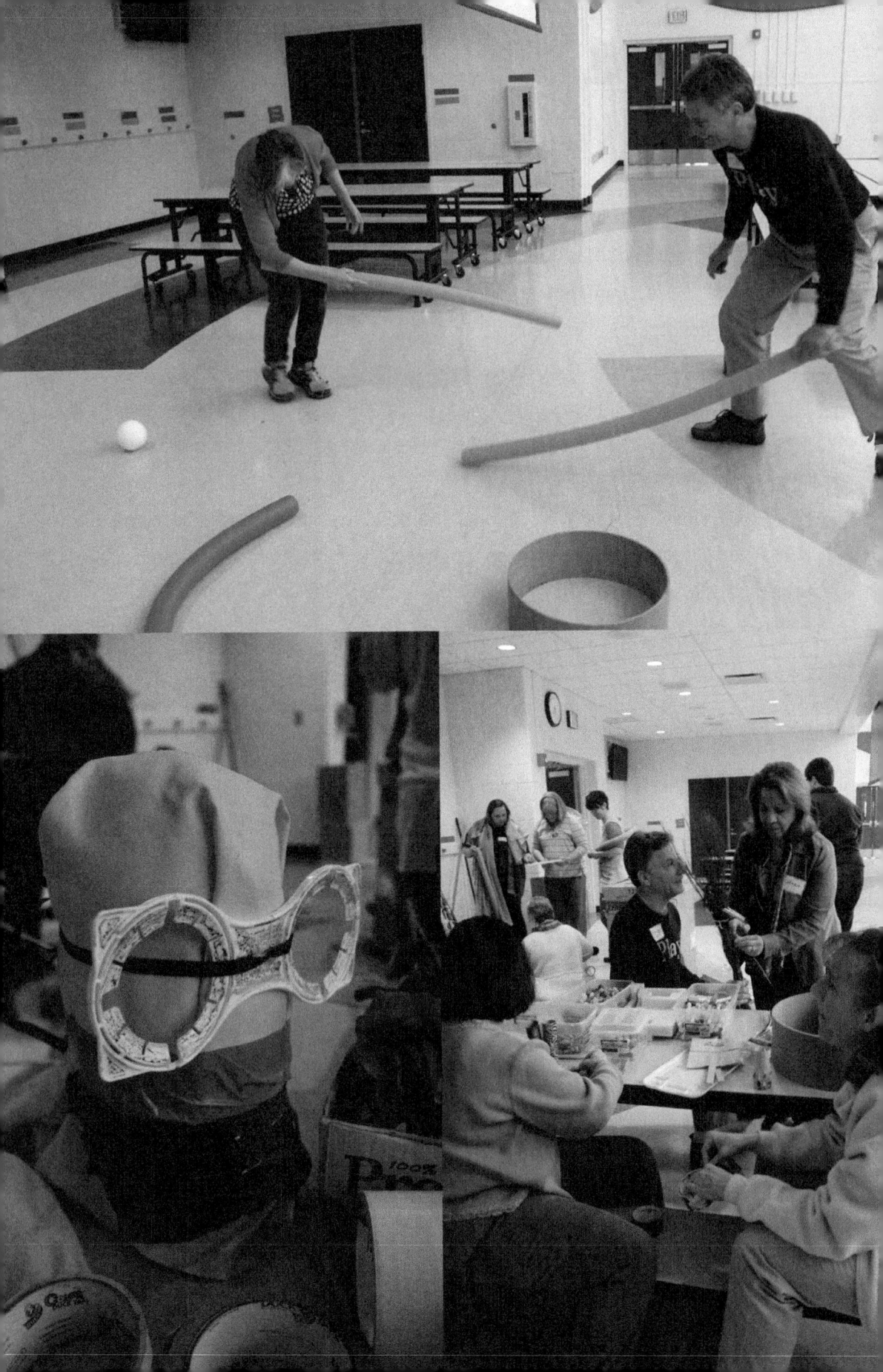

Pandora Redwin: The Play Workshop, Northampton, MA

Pandora lives in rural Western Massachusetts with her partner and daughter, and has been delivering pop-up adventure playgrounds in the Northampton area for the past year.

'I grew up a farm kid whose entire childhood was a constant round of big adventure play on rambling wild acres. Themes in relation to nature, freedom, responsibility, risk, trust and creative, open-ended play are rooted on that farm for me, and the playwork movement has provided the perfect vehicle for moving these themes forward. Pop-up adventure playgrounds created an instant tie in to childhood for many adults, and an opportunity for kids to immediately shine as experts. If (adults) don't immediately link to their own childhood freedoms, they usually ask "What *is* this?" But the kids never seem to ask "What is this?" They just say, "Can we come in yet?" The kids know exactly what to do'.

What they do is what children always will do given the opportunity: they will build and create, imagine and experiment; in other words, play.

'We had boats in a water fountain, sinking and floating both. We had robots and extended room cardboard villages, "traps", cars and devices that slung 4 inch tree "cookies" up a tall sloping sculpture to be caught by the repurposed bike tube and sent flying again. We had zoos and seesaws, arches and binoculars. We had a sloping cannon-looking thing for leaping into a corral of hay. We had the whole world made again every time, kid size and glorious.'

Pandora has long-term plans for a fixed adventure playground, but she also wants to spark a broader conversation surrounding various difficult issues, such risk and freedom. So far, the response has been extremely positive.

'It's been green lights everywhere. The Play Workshop has been lucky enough to be burgeoning during a bit of a playwork/child-directed play/adventure playground national media blitz, and there is no doubt that has helped to swell the interest in what we are up to. Maybe it is the perfect time in the perfect place, but we have had nothing but a thankful, excited and ready-to-get-engaged public response.'

Of course, she knows that, once the conversation turns towards hammers and saws, this might change; nevertheless, she says firmly, 'I'm ready for whatever comes'.

CHAPTER TWO

A couple of hundred miles into the tour, it became clear that our little car was missing certain luxuries, such as power locks, electric windows, a working CD player and air conditioning. The landscape distracted us from such discomforts, offering a rolling scene of mountains rising before cascading into flats, of deserts that burst into a sudden canyon of candy-striped buttes. There was a fountain full of pink plastic flamingos, their knees coquettishly bent, outside of a desert gas station. We'd eaten lunch in middle-of-nowhere parking lots with views of a whole mountain range. Pulling into Lubbock, Texas we saw miles upon miles of blackness with tiny blinking red lights; what we thought could be an alien invasion actually turned out to be a large-scale wind farm.

The landscape was surreal, and my conversation didn't help: as the car's Resident American I was asked to explain the places we passed through. Based on my memories of middle-school history classes and John Denver lyrics, we discussed similarities between the Appalachians and the Welsh Valleys. We covered four locations with Grant—from Ithaca, NY through Texas—before dropping him off in Los Angeles. A couple of days later, we were back there at the airport to collect Andy.

At each stop, our hosts were thrilled to see us arrive. They ran out of their houses with their arms open. They fed us dinner, put us up in their spare rooms, and shared the best of their cities. Over those dinner tables, there'd been long and heartfelt conversations, and more than one host had cried. 'I felt so alone for so long,' one had said, 'but I don't now'. There was a sense that these had been dark times for play advocates, and that parts of childhood once taken for granted now seemed almost forgotten.

I was talking about how playworkers assess risk, and used the example of a child climbing a tree. Shudders went through the audience.

'We could never, never let children climb the trees,' a woman called from the third row.

'Oh,' I said. 'Okay.' I started talking about hammocks, but was soon corrected. You couldn't hang anything from a tree in this part of California either, apparently, nor could you gently lean things against them or drape pieces of yarn from their branches. 'So the rule is, really, no...'

'No fun,' the same woman said, flatly. 'The rule is no fun with the trees. Ever.'

For a country that cares so much about rights, I thought, we sure let some important ones go.

MONEY TALK: BUDGETS AND INSURANCE

People were generous with their advice, both on our driving routes and our budget. Some were concerned only that Suzanna and I not pay for this venture ourselves, while others were baffled we didn't seek large-scale corporate funding.

Deciding a project's budget and scope is a delicate process, and there are always compromises that must be made. There's only one thing that has to be right from the beginning: people.

Those relationships that are built with the nearby children and adults, and with other local organisations, are a vital part of playwork practice. Many people have great instincts for play support, but everyone needs training in order to become a playworker. It's easy to miss how important this work is, simply because doing it well involves great subtlety.

Our workshops addressed the basics of playwork, showing where these ideas come from and how they might be applied in an effort to help improve any setting—and on any budget.

The first question was almost always the same. A person would put up their hand and then looked embarrassed, mumbling, 'I don't want to be *that* person, but how on earth do these places get insurance?'

Maayan Bar-Yam has been enthusiastic about adventure playgrounds since he was a teenager, and we met during his tour of UK adventure playgrounds. In 2014, Cambridge hired him to conduct a feasibility study on the idea of opening a new adventure playground.

'When I spoke with three of the five people in the United States who have actually gotten adventure playgrounds started, they all told me insurance was the least of their problems. Insurance companies are not actually so afraid of adventure playgrounds, presumably because they are staffed by trained playworkers who really know what they are doing. If you think about it, the things kids do on adventure playgrounds are not all that different from the kinds of things kids do at summer camp.'

It's true: skydiving clubs and sword-swallowing classes get insurance. Why not adventure playgrounds?

We also found that, for people starting out with pop-up adventure playgrounds, another local organisation can often be persuaded to partner with your event and put it under their umbrella policy. What's more, developing such community links can help strengthen the project through the inclusion of new people with experiences and resources different to your own—even turning strangers into friends.

KEY PLAYERS

Craig Langlois: Berkshire Museum, Pittsfield, MA

Craig Langlois is Education and Public Programme Manager at the Berkshire Museum—the mission of which is to bring together art, history and natural science. We launched the tour from their second annual Ten Days of Play celebration, this year coinciding with what the weather reports referred to as 'snowpocalypse'. We battled through the heavy drifts, and saw people quickly carrying cardboard in and out so it wouldn't get wet. In a town muffled by snow, their Crane Room—normally used to host funders—was raucous with robots, pirate ships and enthusiastic hollering.

'I wanted an opportunity for children to be in charge and be children. I wanted to offer an opportunity for people to disconnect, to turn off the screens and for parents and supporting members of the community to be pushed just a little bit outside their comfort zone,' said Craig. He kindly shared some comments from visitors:

'My child hasn't sat and focused on one thing for more than 15 minutes since he could walk. We have been here for three hours.'

'This has been a great experience for our daughter. She has had trouble connecting with her peers. Now she has invited the entire Crane Room to her birthday party!'

'Thank you, thank you, thank you! This is just the type of family outing we needed. Please, please, please do it again!'

'It has been great to see my son disconnect from his computer and connect back with himself!' This is our second day of play. Last night our living room became a castle, row boat, spaceship that can only be used if you are wearing a magical robe made out of the burlap sacks you let us take home yesterday.'

'We came up from Connecticut after our friends told us what a great time they had. We have not laughed this much together in a long time.'

Craig has been a huge advocate for free play at the museum, and has championed this extended pop-up adventure playground for years. The Crane Room was due for renovation, and Craig had cleverly arranged for the wall-to-wall cardboard matting to be laid two weeks early so that the antique floors would be protected from crushed felt tip pens and tape. Although he had other responsibilities, he kept sneaking down to see what was going on.

'It looks, feels and sounds like total chaos. But, if you stop, watch and listen for even just a few seconds, you realise that what seems like chaos is really controlled in an innate, primitive, shared creative way. It helps me apply that same thinking when I work with students or play with my son; to step back and observe what's really joining on, give up my desire to fix, and just support in the best way possible.'

Jeremiah Dockray and Erica Larsen: Eureka Villa, Santa Clarita, CA

In a town called Val Verde, located within Los Angeles county, an oddly shaped piece of land is waiting—a former public park Jeremiah started exploring as part of a homework assignment for the Playworker Development Course.

He'd been interested in playwork for years, discovering it through the work of British Anarchist (and adventure playground enthusiast) Colin Ward. 'It weaves together many things that I am passionate about; play, social justice, education, civil rights, community issues...' he said. For Erica, adventure playgrounds appeal because they run counter to the rest of their neighbourhood, which is 'rife with over-scheduled, and over-schooled, over-worked kids and adults'.

They started off by experimenting with pop-up adventure playgrounds: 'They have allowed us to broaden our efforts to reach a larger spectrum of families, and also gave us a wonderful way to "get our feet wet", test out different ideas and practice our playworking in an environment that is less formal while simultaneously educating the public.'

And the public's response? 'Amazing! Everyone thinks we are geniuses,' says Jeremiah. 'The excitement and buzz that sweeps over any pop-up we do is contagious and invigorating both for the kids and adults.' Erica agrees, adding that 'The pop-ups are soul food for sure'.

Jeremiah, Erica and their son Dallas took us out to see the land. There were big trees and bushy, overgrown shrubs. There was a squash plant that produced squash the exact size and colour of tennis balls, and squirrels had been storing them up in the palm trees. There were several large stone fireplaces, and a few ropes that suggested local children had been playing here already. Buying land to begin an adventure playground is a *huge* undertaking for anyone, and Erica and Jeremiah are now knee-deep in paperwork to form their new organisation.

It may not be easy, but it is rewarding.

'This work has given me a much-needed dose of perspective,' says Jeremiah. Erica teaches art and says that her methods have been 'totally transformed' by these experiences. Learning more about playwork 're-validated much of the personal impulses I've had to be more hands off and just let kids explore'. Most importantly, she stated, 'Our home has become more playful, our relationship with our 4 year old son Dallas has bloomed greatly, and our play together is rich and loving'.

CHAPTER THREE

The first month we drove from winter to summer, and the next we drove back again; into the cold mornings huffing out clouds; into the snow. We reached up into the roof box and pulled out coats that hardly looked familiar. At the next stop, we pulled out scarves and hats, sighing.

All our guests had been and gone. Grant, a vegetarian in Texas, had subsisted on fried pickles, and Andy had driven us through the redwoods like it was a race car track. Erin joined us 'for one night only' in Philadelphia, where we talked outside and she projected scenes from her documentary onto a billowing bedsheet we'd brought with us. Now, it was Suzanna and me, with 2,124 miles to drive in 3 days if we were to reach Chicago in time.

This was a time of sleep, drive, sleep, drive. Having played every single car game and having talked about everything we'd ever seen or done or thought, the two of us grew peculiar. Our best game was Yellow Car FM. To play, the passenger acted as DJ using the stereo and adopting a funny voice. I had a pile of unlabelled songs on my phone, so plugged it in, said, 'This one goes out to the lonely hearts', and played what turned out to be theme from the Golden Girls. Suzanna laughed so hard she started to cry. She opened her timeslot with the theme from Mulan and looked at me meaningfully, then ended her show by telling the story of The Little Yellow Car to the background of swelling classical music. It would have been touching had it not been so funny: I laughed until I thought I might be sick.

Our check engine light had been blinking intermittently since we started, and we'd passed so many shredded tires on the freeway that the car's continued survival seemed miraculous. Both of us were half-delirious from fatigue, and I'd drunk so much coffee I could smell it rising from my pores, but we held together.

In Omaha, we stayed with a student on the course named Teal. She asked to see our map, now marked up and made fragile by a thousand unfoldings. We pointed out favourite spots and explained how momentum had been growing.

We'd started a gift box system, where each host put together a collection of junk from their event and sent it to the next. Suzanna posted the pictures to our Facebook page, and soon the people we'd just met started talking with the people we were headed towards. Suzanna had taken that one step further and begun match-making hosts with others doing similar work.

'You're like the Johnny Appleseeds of play,' Teal said. I laughed, and then turned to explain this to Suzanna, who grinned in approval.

RISK AND INCLUSION/PUBLIC ACCESS

Good adventure playgrounds are always a little different from one another, simply because they are expressions of the interests and needs of the people who build them. No site is 'pure' because every project involves some compromise. No site has all the money, staff or land it could desire. Or perhaps those aren't really problems at all, whereas children's access to the site is. Whatever the local situation, however, playworkers are careful to tailor their response in line with their ultimate goal: to meet children where they are—whether in a school or a public park.

It may sound unusual to have an adventure playground on school grounds, particularly a school for children with developmental and linguistic differences who tend to be even more over-protected than others; however, Margaret Noecker, former Houston Adventure Playground Association Board member and Head of The Parish School, insisted that *all* children need opportunities for challenging, risky, creative play. She has sadly passed since, but her legacy continues.

Parish's adventure playground serves the children who attend its after-school programme. However, as opposed to worksheets and board games, they get to build shelters with real tools and develop elaborate games of pretend. AP opened with 8 students in 2008, and now, one-third of all age-eligible children participate. It is arguably a private adventure playground, but this 'privacy' allows for freedoms that otherwise may not have been afforded.

Ithaca Children's Garden, on the other hand, is located within a public park, meaning they are fully accessible from dawn until dusk, every day of the year. Over time, this has meant changes in the materials left out overnight and those put away; every year they have more junk, and more of it is there for the public to enjoy, even when staff aren't around. Furthermore, their mission of environmental education has informed their playwork practice and inspired richer plantings and a more diverse wildlife habitat than I have rarely seen elsewhere.

We are living in a period of hyper-awareness regarding risk. Disproportionate fears and alarmist language on the television would have an alien visitor convinced that human children are made of glass. The truth is, children are usually perfectly happy bouncing around and getting a little bruised; it is we adults that freak out. It's vitally important to engage with parents and caregivers, and to invite them to play as well—adults who play are more able to recognise its benefits for their children, and to support the process without accidentally making it their own. Having parents onside is key for any modern adventure playground.

On the other hand, however, children also need time away from their parents. They need to make new friends and get into a little mischief. Playworkers find ways to help create that space, whether by working with parents directly or by taking time to explain that staff are highly trained professionals. Copies of the site's risk/benefit assessment forms and other documentation often help when making the case for free play to funders, administrators and community members.

KEY PLAYERS

Jill Wood: Parish School, Houston, TX

Jill was Head Librarian when assigned the task of opening an adventure playground. It is now a bustling site, rich with evidence of play, but at the beginning it was an empty field with two cement culvert pipes and a large info binder from the now-defunct Houston Adventure Playground Association.

'When I first read about playwork, I was enormously grateful that smart, disciplined people had named things that were intuitive for me. We adults, who prioritise child-defined worlds and agendas, need a way to talk to one another. And we need language to communicate with other adults in children's lives—parents, teachers, city planners, playground designers, doctors.'

Those people often ask about their safety record; with all these risks, surely it couldn't be safe? In fact, over the past seven years, they've had lots of bruises but 'no broken bones or stitches yet'. The traditional, fixed-equipment playground has seen two broken arms in two years—even though children spend perhaps half as much time there as they do on AP. Jill explains that it's because 'there is a sense of ownership over the space that allows children to know every inch of the playground; 'allows them to take individualised, graduated risks and know themselves through that process'.

From books to scrap may seem a strange leap, but, as Jill commented; 'Play always made sense to me. Probably because I'm an anxious person by nature, and the context of play takes the pressure off. No performance, no product—just the present and process. When I started our adventure playground, the freedom and anonymity of the space was exhilarating, as was the satisfaction of creating a safe place for children, many of whom are also anxious because they don't fit easily into the world as it is designed.'

Here, however, children are able to design it for themselves. They build forts and stables for their 'horses', and leave places deliberately undesigned, such as the field they call 'the Great Unknown'.

Her experiences and studies have changed the way that Jill looks at the world. 'I began our adventure playground thinking it would be a creative, positive outlet for students at The Parish School—icing on the cake, if you will. Seven years later, I am worried about how unique our space is. I don't see children skateboarding, kicking around a ball or bicycling in the street when I come home from work. I live in a residential neighbourhood, in the centre of the United States' fourth largest city, and I don't see children.'

At the time of writing, Jill and her husband Patrick have begun hosting pop-up adventure playgrounds beyond the Parish School's boundaries...

Erin Marteal: Hands-on-Nature Anarchy Zone, public garden

Erin started at Ithaca Children's Garden as a volunteer and is now its director. The Garden is three acres of wetland and meadow, visited by nesting birds and muddy snakes, as well as more human visitors. A few years ago, in partnership with Rusty Keeler (author of *Natural Playscapes*) and US Fish & Wildlife, they opened the Hands-on-Nature Anarchy Zone.

In the beginning, all was mud. Their first annual Mud Day celebrations involved truckloads of talc-smooth topsoil and a good hosing down by the Fire Department. The mud sank and bubbled, becoming smooth as chocolate pudding. Since then, they've been adding shovels, climbing ropes, muffin trays, construction hats, with many of these materials donated by community members, including a full catering set that arrived one night.

Erin's vision was 'of a place where kids of all ages, but particularly older children, would be free to build, construct, create, dream, and get filthy, away from the watchful adult eyes'. This meant accepting the ugly beauty of a good adventure playground, and believing others would, too. Sometimes conflicts arise between different projects being run within the same garden, but a gold thread of loving children's play runs through all of the work of the staff, which they use to help them make decisions as they go.

'The playwork practice was a natural complement to what we were offering in the physical space, and we felt it was a key piece to really make the space and project successful,' Erin said. 'Once we became familiar with playwork—and, even more so, when we began formal training in playwork—we breathed a collective sigh of relief. "Aaah... So *that's* what you do when....".'

They've been doing a series of off-site events, directly reaching into local communities. 'Families, schools, community centres and children have been extremely receptive,' Erin says. They've also been receiving attention from farther afield, as Rusty made a guest appearance with Erin Davis on the Katie Couric Show. There have been lots of physical changes as well, with new plantings and projects witnessed every season.

Maintaining this state of 'constant evolution' is a great deal of work, but the process itself has helped Erin Marteal find a balance.

'As adults—and particularly as American adults—we tend to place an extraordinary premium on work work work. Play is completely overshadowed. This particular focus has helped me pull that back, both in terms of creating a work environment that is joyful and playful, as well as bringing play into my own personal life.'

CHAPTER FOUR

Suzanna flew out of Boston. During the tour, people had often asked us, 'Aren't you two sick of each other yet?' and the answer to that question would always be the same: no. Without her presence, the car felt very quiet.

Everyone had taken their luggage, and it turned out the car went like a rocket when empty. I patted her on the dashboard and apologised for those unkind words when we'd climbed mountains in second gear. The roof box was still on, and when a truck went past the wind caught it and nearly blew me into the ditch.

It takes time to process a trip such as this, but even now, the memories slide over one another and refuse to reconcile. It's a cliché to say there are many Americas; if that's true, we've seen only a few. People keep asking us what we saw, what we learned. I learned something difficult to pinpoint; something about the scale of the country itself and of our own potential. With such a question in mind, however, I have identified some of my lessons from the road:

We're all much braver than we know

So many parents are not afraid of their children climbing trees but *are* afraid of being judged by other parents. Hosts told us that their biggest surprise was meeting so many people who agreed with them, who wanted to help make change happen but didn't know how.

Similarly, we led a workshop in a park and recreation setting where the Director wanted more emphasis on play, as did frontline staff. In fact, they'd been sneaking opportunities to incorporate free play into their schedules for ages, keeping it a secret. Once in the same room, we realised the barrier had been formed by risk-averse middle management.

The processes of analysing risk, as well as the vocabulary that allows us to distinguish between different types of risk, is incredibly helpful: it reminds us how many risks we take daily. Every time we get into the car or fall in love, we're taking a serious risk—and fear alone is no reason to quit something you feel moved to do.

Great things happen in small communities

Part of the ambition with this tour was to visit people outside of major metropolitan areas, both to see what was going on locally and to help them feel more connected. What astonished me were the stories of local organisations and tireless individuals doing amazing things each and every day. What's more, the local authorities in smaller towns are often more open to new ideas: as one organiser said, 'Our town nearly went bust, and since then it's been like the land that bureaucracy forgot. I think they're just so glad that people want to stay and try something new...'

After our workshop in Portland, we were thrilled to see a line of people waiting with questions. Our host said, 'I have wanted to open an adventure playground for years, but can't imagine where to find land around here'. Moments later, a lady shuffled over to us to explain that she had a plot of land available, and Suzanna's eyes lit up. We shepherded the two parties together and then stepped back. A playworker uses a light touch.

It's always the same, and it's always different

Whether you interpret it as an evolutionary adaptation or simply a celebration of life itself, play comes from a place deep within us—deeper than language and even species. Other animals play, too, and anyone who has thrown a stick for a dog knows how to read the cues that ask, *Will you play with me?*

The expression of this instinct, however, differs every single time. You would think that, after a few dozen pop-up adventure playgrounds, we'd have seen everything that can be done to a cardboard box, but no. Every single play session, every workshop, offers a surprise.

There are people in every corner of this country doing wonderful things to make children's right to play a reality. By turning off the news and going outside, we're more able to meet each other and start building the playful communities we want to live in—together!

Thank you, everyone, for helping to make this experience so extraordinary. I'll carry it with me always.

Love,
Morgan

FAQs

Our workshops are always conversational, and people are welcome to interrupt us at any time. However, at the end of each talk, we thank people for their attention and ask if they have any questions. Since that's rather more difficult in book form, here are answers to the questions we are Most Frequently Asked during the tour.

'Ummm, I don't want to be *that person* but what about liability?'
Liability or insurance issues *can* be tricky, but are not insurmountable (Chapter 2). One way is to avoid the word 'playground' entirely when talking about a fixed or permanent site. Public playgrounds have to meet specific guidelines, whereas other forms of provision often do not. For events, you can usually either partner with a sympathetic museum or library, or work with the park's department to come under their policy.

Remember: it's not the hammers and nails that make an adventure playground; rather, it's children's freedom and sense of ownership. If you find yourself getting stuck, we recommend finding ways around the block, rather than beating your head against it.

'So, adventure playgrounds sound great, but how are they possible in America?'
The USA has its own particular challenges (Chapter 3), but they are not unique. We get emails from adventure playground enthusiasts all around the world, and whether they're writing from Israel or Italy, they still ask first about liability: 'over-protective' parents, and adults' dislike of mess and noise, etc.

These issues are *why* adventure playgrounds exist in the first place: so that children have somewhere to escape to. However, it's important to respect the concerns of local residents and parents or caregivers. The social importance of having clean, quality clothes should never be ridiculed, nor should fears of physical injury. As one audience member said to Andy, 'It's alright for you to talk about risk when, in your country, a broken arm gets taken care of by the NHS. Here, it could bankrupt a family.'

However, broken limbs are rarer on adventure playgrounds than on fixed-equipment sites because children can explore risk slowly and carefully (rather than climbing the outside of equipment that wasn't designed with this in mind).

'You talk a lot about freedom, but doesn't it become like *Lord of the Flies*?'

No, it doesn't. Children are people, and most people are basically very decent to one another. *Lord of the Flies* is fiction—a parable of human darkness and an adult fantasy—not a documentary.

Freedom is crucial for play. The word is often framed as 'freedom from', such as from fear or persecution, for example. On a playground, these might mean freedom from adult pressures to achieve or perform; from our own expectations of their behaviour or preferences or goals.

Just as important are children's 'freedoms to': the freedom to run, to sit, to breathe the open air. Children need freedom to claim their time as their own and do with it as they please, to make friends and negotiate those friendships themselves. Asking, 'What are children free to do here?' should be a regular part of managing any site.

When trusted with their own freedom, children demonstrate extraordinary kindness. Of course, conflict is inevitable within any community, but children need opportunities to practice dealing with conflict themselves. Staff are there if children want to talk or seek mediation. If you're in a setting where children have had very few opportunities to become accustomed to their freedoms, materials should be chosen that allow them to practice.

Foam pool noodles, for example, offer a great way for children to practice rough-and-tumble play. New materials can then be introduced slowly, as they grow more skilled in both the social and material aspects of play.

'Why is play so important?'

Play is part of life! Play can be fun, challenging, sociable or solitary. Play can include watching the clouds, splashing in water, construction and demolition. Play is simultaneously as unique as every individual while also being something that connects us all.

Play is essential for health and happiness, irrespective of how old or young you are, but a child's need to play is particularly acute for their cognitive development, emotional wellbeing, socialisation and more (Guildbaud, 2008). However, in order to maintain a focus on play as children's right, playworkers call these 'windfall benefits' (Powell *et al.*, 2008). This means that these benefits are real, but no child has said, 'It's time for some gross motor development'. Children play because they long to—and that ought to be enough.

In fact, play is so important that playworkers tend to talk not in terms of play's benefits but rather of the consequences of its deprivation. The loss of play opportunities has been linked with a range of issues, including depression, worsening symptoms of ADHD, and autistic spectrum disorder, amongst others (Panksaap, 2007; Louv, 2010). The most common issues we see amongst play-deprived children are aggression and social withdrawal, from which children can heal themselves with enough time, space and practice.

It is also worth reflecting on the importance of play in adults' lives, as well as in the lives of our communities. Stuart Brown's 2010 book *Play: How it Shapes the Brain, Opens the Imagination and Invigorates the Soul* demonstrates that we all need play—regardless of our age. For adults, play might include singing in the car or spending time with friends, knitting or going salsa dancing.

Play is also essential for rebuilding communities. In community-building, there is a concept of the 'third place', which infers somewhere that is not home or work, but which is welcoming and friendly. In his 1989 book *The Great Good Place*, Ray Oldenburg describes these places as being many different things: free or inexpensive; often including food or drink; accessible by foot; including 'regulars'; welcoming and comfortable; and a place where people can find old friends and new. For children, playgrounds and spaces that fit these criteria are an essential part of their cultural life; they are where they meet one another, share stories and information, and, of course, have marvellous adventures.

'I have to talk with parents/policy makers/sceptics regularly as part of my work. How can I persuade them that this is a good way to go?'
Advocating and engaging with adult agendas is a big part of playwork practice (Appendix)—and sometimes the most challenging! It can be frustrating to talk with people whose priorities and viewpoints are so radically different from your own. Often, their concerns are based on fear or misunderstanding—situations where everyone want the best for children but disagree on what that might look like. These conversations can become emotional, simply because we are all invested in our own ideas.

Preparation is key. Therefore, it is pivotal to find out as much as you can about the audience, their goals and priorities. Play has been studied across many disciplines, and its benefits are so plentiful that you can make the case for play on nearly any grounds—behavioural, educational, community cohesion, and so forth. Gather both stories *and* statistics in an effort to reach them in the head and the heart. Also, find and nurture relationships with members of those communities and ask for their help. Sometimes, it's a matter of learning the right vocabulary for the crowd in order to put these ideas in ways they understand.

When it is impossible to persuade, you can also navigate. Spots of time can be carved out from other programming and opened to play. When all else fails, I engage domineering parents in small talk: 'I love your shirt, where did you get it?' will often get them to chat with me, while their child gets five minutes to themselves.

'You keep talking about playwork. How do I learn more about it?'
It won't come as a surprise at this point to say that we *love* playwork. For both Suzanna and I, it is more than a profession: like play itself, playwork can be understood as an approach to life—one that can be extraordinarily rewarding for the practitioner. It takes time, study and practice to become a playworker, and the task of self-improvement is never complete.

We've gathered some websites to help you get started. We also designed and delivered the Playworker Development Course—a 12-module distance learning foundation in playwork practice. Students are currently taking this course in 12 countries, with those enrolled including teachers, therapists, parents, community aid workers and more. Their experiences bringing more opportunities for play into these diverse settings have taught us a great deal about flexibility, nuance and opportunism. You can find out more about this course by visiting our website.

'You keep talking about risk! Where do I learn more about that?'
Risk and challenge are central topics in playwork—not because they are any

more important than other aspects of play, but because children have fewer opportunities to enjoy them. One phrase you'll often hear is 'risk-benefit assessment', particularly in the further readings listed below. Risk/benefits assessments encompass a range of both formal and informal tools playworkers use every day to help remove hazards (meaning true dangers without benefits, such as broken glass) while retaining challenges (such as things to climb or balance on).

In an example of tree-climbing, the risk of injury by falling is weighed against the benefits of climbing. Those benefits include a sense of accomplishment, of height and quiet, and perhaps some social cachet. For playworkers, the need is to mitigate against dangers while still allowing a behaviour to take place, such as by throwing crash pads underneath the branches, for example. If children cannot take risks safely, where there are first aid-trained members of staff, they will take them *unsafely* and out of sight of adults.

We view risk as simply part of life. Every time we cross the road, introduce ourselves to a stranger, change jobs or form new relationships, we weigh benefits against risks and make our choice accordingly. This is precisely why we want to help children to gain the opportunities they need to practice risks, to learn, and to expand their own limits—all at their own pace. Children need chances to face the challenges they create, to achieve their goals and to survive disappointment. If we want our children to be brave, resilient and determined, we have to let them take risks.

'This all sounds awesome! How do I get started in my own neighbourhood?'
This is a favourite question, and the answer is simple—just get in contact with us! If you're interesting in hosting your own pop-up adventure playground, there's a little form to complete on our website. If you want to

work towards a permanent site, get in touch and we'll talk about some different models and options to help you find the right path for you, the children, and your community.

Morgan (morgan@popupadventureplay.org)

Suzanna (suzanna@popupadventureplay.org)

LET'S STAY IN TOUCH

We hope you liked this book. We loved making it.

If you'd like to get in touch with any of the wonderful people who we have mentioned in this book, please get in contact with us.

If you're interested in learning more about playwork, the Appendix provides the Playwork Principles.

Furthermore, in mind of future editions, we would love to improve our knowledge on the short history of adventure playgrounds in the USA and to connect with previous playwork generations, so if you have more information on this, please do get in touch!

USEFUL RESOURCES

Websites

www.playengland.org.uk

www.playwales.org.uk

www.playscotland.org

www.ncb.org.uk/cpis/resources/factsheets

Free Online Readings

Tim Gill (2012). *No Fear*, available via: www.gulbenkian.org.uk.
Penny Wilson (2010). *The Playwork Primer*, available via: www.allianceforchildhood.org/playwork.
Wendy Russell (2006). *Reframing Playwork: Reframing Challenging Behaviour*, available via: http://www.academia.edu/.
Play Safety Forum (2002). *Managing Risk in Play Provision: An Implementation Guide*, available via: http://www.playengland.org.uk/resources/managing-risk-in-play-provision-implementation-guide.aspx.

Recommended Books (Worth the Purchase!)

Almon, J. (2013). Adventure—The Value of Risk in Children's Play. CreateSpace Independent Publishing Platform.
Bengtsson, A. (1972). Adventure Playgrounds. Crosby Lockwood: London
Brown, F. & Taylor, C. (2008). Foundations of Playwork. Open University Press.
Brown, F. (2014). Play and Playwork 101 Stories of Children Playing. Open University Press.
Else, P. (2009). The Value of Play. Continuum.
Hughes, B. (2011). Evolutionary Playwork. Routledge.
Kilvington, J. & Wood, A. (2010). *Reflective Playwork: For all who work with children.* London: Continuum.

APPENDIX

PLAYWORK PRINCIPLES

These principles were developed by playworkers across the UK and have been endorsed by SkillsActive in 2004. More information on the process can be found on the SkillsActive website, available at the following URL: www.skillsactive.com/playwork/principles.

The Principles establish the professional and ethical framework for playwork, and therefore must be regarded as a whole. They describe what is unique about play and playwork, and provide the playwork perspective for working with children and young people.

They are based on the recognition that children's and young people's capacity for positive development will be enhanced if given access to the broadest range of environments and play opportunities.

1. All children and young people need to play. The impulse to play is innate. Play is a biological, psychological and social necessity, and is fundamental to the healthy development and wellbeing of individuals and communities.

2. Play is a process that is freely chosen, personally directed and intrinsically motivated; that is, children and young people determine and control the content and intent of their play by following their own instincts, ideas and interests, in their own way and for their own reasons.

3. The prime focus and essence of playwork is on supporting and facilitating the play process, and this should inform the development of play policy, strategy, training and education.

4. For playworkers, the play process takes precedence, and

playworkers act as advocates for play when engaging with adult-led agendas.

5. The role of the playworker is centred on supporting all children and young people in the creation of a space in which they can play.

6. The playworker's response to children and young people playing is based on a sound, up-to-date knowledge of the play process and reflective practice.

7. Playworkers recognise their own impact on the play space, and also the impact of children and young people's play on the playworker.

8. Playworkers choose an intervention style that enables children and young people to extend their play. All playworker intervention must balance risk with the developmental benefit and wellbeing of children.

Playwork Principles Scrutiny Group 2004

REFERENCES

A SHORT HISTORY OF ADVENTURE PLAYGROUNDS

Bengtsson, A. (1972). *Adventure Playgrounds.* London, Crosby Lockwood.

Bertelsen, J. (1972). Early Experience in Emdrup. In: *Adventure Playgrounds.* London, Crosby Lockwood, pp. 16–23.

Bosselmann, P. (1998). Landscape Architecture as art: C. Th. Sorensen, a humanist. Landscape Journal, 17(1): 62–69.

DCSF (2008). The Play Strategy. Available from: <http://webarchive.nationalarchives.gov.uk/20130401151715/http://www.edu cation.gov.uk/publications/eOrderingDownload/The_Play_Strategy.pdf> [Accessed January 14, 2015].

Meynell Games (2015). The National Playwork Conference [Internet]. Available from: <http://www.playworkconferences.org.uk/> [Accessed January 14, 2015].

Ward, C. (1978). *The Child in the City.* Pantheon Books.

Ward, C. (1982). *Anarchy in action.* London, Freedom Press.

ADVENTURE PLAYGROUNDS IN THE USA

Bengtsson, A. (1972), *Adventure Playgrounds.* London, Crosby Lockwood.

Benjamin, J. (1974). *Grounds for Play.* Oxford, Bedford Square Press.

Frost, J.L. (2009). *A History of Children's Play and Play Environments: Toward a Contemporary Child-Saving Movement.* Routledge.

PLAYWORK PRINCIPLES

Brown, F. (2008). The Playwork Principles: A critique. In: F. Brown & C. Taylor eds. *Foundations of Playwork.* Maidenhead, Open University Press/McGraw Hill, pp. 123–127.

PPSG (2005). Playwork Principles. Play Wales. Available from: <http://www.playwales.org.uk/login/uploaded/documents/Playwork%20Princi ples/playwork%20principles.pdf> [Accessed May 19, 2013].

CHAPTER ONE

Baldegg, K.C.-M. von (2014). Inside a European Adventure Playground [Internet]. Available from: <http://www.theatlantic.com/video/archive/2014/03/europes-adventure-playgrounds-look-way-more-fun/284521/> [Accessed September 10, 2014].
Davis, E. (2014). Playfreemovie.com [Internet]. Available from: <http://playfreemovie.com/> [Accessed July 11, 2014].
O'Connor, T. (2015). Lake Erie Adventure Play—LEAP [Internet]. Available from: <https://www.facebook.com/lakeerieadventureplay> [Accessed January 16, 2015].
Putnam, R. D. (2001). *Bowling Alone: The Collapse and Revival of American Community.* New Jersey, Simon and Schuster.
Redwin, P. (2015). The Play Workshop [Internet]. Available from: <http://www.theplayworkshop.com/> [Accessed January 16, 2015].

CHAPTER TWO

Berkshire Museum (2015). Berkshire Museum. Available from: <http://berkshiremuseum.org/> [Accessed January 16, 2015].
Larsen, E. & Jeremiah, D. (2014). Santa Clarita Adventure Play [Internet]. Available from: <http://scvadventureplay.com/> [Accessed January 16, 2015].

CHAPTER THREE

Ithaca Children's Garden (2015). Ithaca Children's Garden [Internet]. Available from: <http://ithacachildrensgarden.org/> [Accessed January 16, 2015].
KAC Productions LLC (2014). Are We Overprotecting Our Kids? *Katie Couric.* Available from: <http://katiecouric.com/2014/07/09/are-we-overprotecting-our-kids/> [Accessed July 21, 2014].
Keeler, R. (2008). *Natural Playscapes.* Redmond, Wash, Exchange Press.
The Parish School (2015). Advancing Language. Empowering Learners. | The Parish School [Internet]. Available from: <http://parishschool.org/> [Accessed January 16, 2015].

CHAPTER FOUR

Brown, S. L. (2010). *Play: How it shapes the brain, opens the imagination, and invigorates the soul.* New York, Avery.

Guildbaud, S. (2003). The Essence of Play. In: F. Brown ed. *Playwork: Theory and Practice.* Maidenhead, England, Open University Press.

Louv, R. (2010). *Last Child in the Woods: Saving our children from nature-deficit disorder.* London, Atlantic.

Oldenburg, R. (1999). *The Great Good Place: Cafes, Coffee Shops, Bookstores, Bars, Hair Salons, and Other Hangouts at the Heart of a Community: Cafes, Coffee Shops... Other Hangouts at the Heart of a Community.* 3rd revised edition. New York : Berkeley, Calif., Marlowe & Co.

Panksepp, J. (2007) Can PLAY Diminish ADHD and Facilitate the Construction of the Social Brain? *Journal of the Canadian Academy of Child and Adolescent Psychiatry*, 16 (2), p. 57.

Powell, S., Wellard, I., National Children's Bureau & Play England (Project) (2008). *Policies and Play: The impact of national policies on children's opportunities for play.* London, National Children's Bureau.

PHOTO CREDITS

Unless otherwise stated, Suzanna Law is the proud owner of all photographs.

The cover photo was taken in Cary, NC, during the Pop-Up Adventure Play and Special Guests Tour 2014.

INTRODUCTION
pp. 6–7: Pop-Up Adventure Playground at Tour Stop #14, hosted by Smith Memorial Playground and Playhouse in Philadelphia, PA.

p. 8: Drive-Thru Tree, Leggitt, CA.

p. 11: Adventure Playground photo, courtesy of Donne Buck.

p. 17: Block Party Pop-Up Adventure Playground in Fairport, NY.

p. 20–22: Pop-Up Adventure Playground at Tour Stop #12, hosted by Be Active Kids in Cary, NC.

p. 25: Clockwise from Top: Hosts from Tour Stop #5 in Santa Clarita, CA. This photo was taken by a family friend, Claude Stephens, host of Tour Stop #3 in Bernheim, KY/the hosts from Tour Stop #12 in Port Clinton, OH/Host, Jill Wood and the AP in The Parish School, Houston, TX. This photo was taken by Patrick Miral.

p. 26: Workshop at Tour Stop #7, hosted by the Civic Innovation Lab at New Children's Museum in San Diego, CA.

p. 28: Top: Map of The Pop-Up Adventure Play and Special Guests Tour 2014, hand drawn. Bottom: Suzanna's travel journal.

p. 32: Top: Erin Davis. Bottom (Left to right): Suzanna Law, Andy Hinchcliffe and Morgan Leichter-Saxby.

p. 33: Top: Suzanna Law, courtesy of Morgan Leichter-Saxby. Bottom left: Grant Lambie. Bottom right: Morgan Leichter-Saxby.

pp. 34–35: Pop-Up Adventure Playground at Tour Stop #9, hosted by Leon Smith of Earthplay and Michelle Mathis of Learning Landscapes Design at Tabor Space, Portland, OR.

CHAPTER ONE
p. 36: Redwood Forest, CA.

pp. 39–41: Pop-Up Adventure Playgrounds at Tour Stop #3, hosted by Bernheim Arboretum and Research Forest in Bernheim Forest, Kentucky.

CPSIA information can be obtained
at www.ICGtesting.com
Printed in the USA
LVOW06s1446211116

513927LV00038B/318/P

9 780956 553997